GIRL – you're all that

Fikile Oyekanmi

GIRL – you're all that

INSPIRED
PUBLISHING

Girl - You're All That

First Edition, First Impression 2019

ISBN 978-0-620-85829-8

Published by:

Inspired Publishing

PO Box 82058 | Southdale | 2135

Johannesburg , South Africa

Email: info@inspiredpublishing.co.za

www.inspiredpublishing.co.za

ACKNOWLEDGEMENT

I am a believer of the statement, "It takes a village to raise a child". I am a product of men and women who stepped into my life, to help, pray, and to guide. There are just too many of you to mention. May you never be stranded in your time of need.

I wrote this book with women in mind. I also wrote it with a special girl in mind, my daughter, Miss Olamide Nompumelelo Oyekanmi. I can't predict what your journey will look like, or what giants you will fight, my baby; all I can say is you already have it in you to WIN therefore "Congratulations", in advance!

To my husband Mr Ademola Oyekanmi and my son Kolawole Wandile Oyekanmi, thank you for adding sugar and spice to my life.

To my family, thank you for your support and always believing in me.

To my friends, I think God went an extra mile in making sure our paths cross. My life is blessed with the best. It is not everyday that one meets people who are so loyal and dependable. Thank you for being the people you are.

To my spiritual covering, Apostle Felix and Pastor Hester Adaeze Okoh, you are truly amazing. Your confidence in me has been the wind beneath my wings. Thank you caring the way you do and for being an example of faith, stability and love. You are the light.

Lastly and most importantly, what can I do without my heavenly Father, God? Thank you for the gift of writing and for the stories of triumph. You have never let go of my hand. I owe my entire being to YOU! I can't thank you enough.

Girl you're All That

CONTENTS

FOREWORD

Dear Reader

This book is dedicated to every beautiful girl and woman on their journey to self-discovery and discovering their worth. It is a journey of hope, love and believing in oneself. Much of the content in this book applies to our lives in some way or the other. It addresses difficult issues we face in our world, while highlighting that God is with us on our journey, inviting us to draw closer to Him, believing in Him and His unconditional love for us all.

The author of this book, Fikile Oyekanmi, is a woman close to God's heart. She is a phenomenal woman of integrity, full of love, compassion, strength and wisdom. She was inspired to write this book relating her personal journey as a young girl child into adolescence. Her passion is to encourage and give hope to every girl and help women to understand their value and worth in a society where we are oftentimes mistreated and misunderstood. Her involvement as part of the women ministry in her local church, is heartfelt.

God has given her a greater vision through her initiative with 'Dance with my Father' where she is the sole founder, allowing young girls and teenagers to experience the love of a father and giving them the foundation to understand how to be respected and treated.

When I read her manuscript for the first time, I was totally blown away by the power of its content. I was transported back to my early life as a young girl and where I am now.

I'm proud to present this book to girls and women of all ages as well as every man that cares to know their daughter, sister, mother and friend better.

"But you are the ones chosen by God, chosen for the high calling of priestly work, chosen to be a holy people, God's instruments to do his work and speak out for Him, to tell others of the night-and-day difference He made for you— from nothing to something, from rejected to accepted".

1 Peter 2:9-10, the Message Bible (MSG)

With love,

Pastor Hester Adaeze Okoh

First Lady, House of Treasures Ministries

& Spiritual mother to the author

INTRODUCTION

The fiercest fight you'll ever fight is the one within you. The silent conversations you have about your dreams, pain, significance, fears, hopes and mistakes. How you go about it makes the difference between ending with a, "Yes I can," or "I am finished".

A popular South African hip hop artist once made a statement that caught my attention. He said, "The world is ready for us to be ourselves".

Many of us are "out there", but in all honesty, we are hiding. We are hiding behind our makeup, fancy clothes, lovely hair, luxury cars, titles, careers, gifts and talents. We flaunt these things to shift the focus off our pain, shame, guilt, discouragement, unforgiveness and a poor self-esteem! We present ourselves with a bounce on the outside, yet internally, we are bent by the heavy load we are dragging.

This book is dedicated to every woman who needs affirmation. Every woman who needs to know that there is no need to hide. I am delighted to share my own journey of dealing with pain, shame, depravation and fighting the negativity that surrounded and still surrounds me. I have seen how leaning on God can lift your head.

I am hoping this book will inspire you to agree with God, and to cooperate with Him. I hope it will inspire you to be your TRUE SELF. That you will be convinced that God sees YOU! Not your imperfections but YOU! He sees YOU from HIS point of view. Wonderfully made! Forgiven! Accepted! Able!

Chapter 1

You Are Not Your Family Background.

Before I shaped you in the womb, I knew all about you. Before you saw the light of day, I had holy plans for you

Jeremiah 1:5 (The Message Bible)

We've heard the statement, "You can choose your friends, but you cannot choose your family". That is true. You had nothing to do with the family you were born into. Some were born into poverty, others affluence. Some grew up around hostility, others in an environment of love. Whatever your case was, childhood experiences can drag into your adult life and either leave you with a sense/feeling of self-worth or low self-esteem. These feelings can determine whether you see yourself as a success or a failure.

I was born in Mzimhlophe, Soweto. My home was a corner house at a street called Ramushu. I am the second born of five children, born from different fathers.

For a greater part of my childhood, no one in my family was employed. I was raised by my maternal grandmother who had no income to take care of me, my four siblings and cousins. When she qualified for old age pension from the state, it became the source of income for my family. We grew up without a father and my mother was also absent most of the time.

There were nights when we went to bed without food. On some days, we would go to our neighbours to ask for mealie meal, sugar, teabags and even bathing soap. Some would give us cheerfully and others would grumble knowing that we may knock again the following day.

Christmas day was no different. If no one had money, we would stay without food. You could accept not having food during the year but not on Christmas day. Christmas day is generally a day for feasting and indulging on every type of food you could not afford to eat the entire year. But not in our home. Christmas day was just another day. More than anything, it was a reminder of how poor we were. There was one year when we ate porridge and pumpkin because that's all we had.

I slept on the kitchen floor because of the size of the house we stayed in (two bedrooms housing about 12 people). I sometimes used soap or salt to brush my teeth and recycled cooking oil for my body because we could not afford toothpaste or body lotion. I faced mockery because of my family's lack.

My mother used to drink alcohol a lot. Everyone in my neighbourhood knew her because her drinking was public knowledge. This just added to the mockery. It used to hurt and embarrass me to see her being carried and escorted by strangers when she was too drunk to walk. I saw how some of her friends and cousins would send her to the tavern to buy alcohol for them. That would be her contribution because most of the time she didn't have money. I overheard how they would talk about her being a 'parasite' for drinking more than all of them despite not having contributed a cent. Witnessing this made me decide that I will never touch alcohol in my life. I hated how it stripped my mother off her dignity. I never hid my dislike of alcohol. My mother and her friends viewed this as being proud. They were quick to tell me that when I was a baby, they used beer to pacify me when I was crying and that I loved it. They further said people like me usually marry drunkards, a statement I always cursed. Though I didn't drink, I didn't escape being labelled, "Umntwana wesidakwa" (child of a drunkard) by one of the adult neighbours. This used to hurt but I could not do anything about it. I could not even report it to anyone at home because this neighbour and my family had a history of animosity. Apparently, she tried to poison my older brother, an incident that led to him having a major operation during his teenage years. My reporting it could have started a fight, which was what I was avoiding especially because she and I attended the same church.

Things were so difficult at home that we could not even get the basics for school, including school shoes. When I owned a pair, it was bought by a teacher or a good Samaritan. I would wear them until they were thoroughly worn out. It was difficult to even raise money for minor repairs to them. I would try all sorts of tricks to keep the soles together including using chewing gum as glue. Obviously, that did not work.

I will never forget being part of the school choir in primary school and not having proper black school shoes. I wore white heels that were given to me by a neighbour. I used to stand at the back so that my shoes wouldn't be a distraction. I remember participating in the school choir competition. We had to walk in a line as we made our way to the stage. The stage floor was wooden. Over and above my shoes being inappropriate and being the wrong colour, they made a distinctive sound that earned me the nickname, "kwaai- kwaai" (this is a township slang word for high heels).

I became a Christian at an early age. I started going to church at the age of 8. My primary reason for going to church was the free bread and soup that we got every Saturday. I belonged to a soup kitchen managed by the Rhema Bible Church in my community. The soup kitchen leader, Mrs Gwendoline Jele, a school principal by profession was the leader of the soup kitchen. She had such a big heart. Over and above teaching us the word of God, giving us soup and sometimes even clothes, she allowed us into her family space. My friend, Tumelo and I clung to her. We became her babies, learning everything from cleaning the house, making a decent cup of tea, leading songs of praise and worship and teaching younger children as we grew older. We called her "MaJacks". Sadly, she was shot and killed in 1999 during an armed robbery at the school where she was the principal.

The moments with MaJacks sowed a seed of the word of God that is still a firm foundation for my life.

Despite all the negative things and circumstances around me, one of the things I was determined to get was an education. I believed that education would give me access to opportunities my family never had. Before my younger brother and I passed Matric, the person who had the highest education in my entire family was my uncle and that was Grade 10, which was called a Junior Certificate ("JC") then. I was determined to break that cycle.

The year MaJacks died was my Matric year. I wrote my exams and failed. This came as a shock to many because I was a top learner whom everyone in school knew. I was part of the team that even organised prayer sessions for Matriculants. Now you can imagine how it felt to be the one failing the exams.

I summoned up the courage to return to the same school the following year and redid my Matric. My courage however didn't come from self- motivation. It came from encouragement from my dear grandmother. She reminded me that I was still very young, and I could do it again. I returned to the same school, needless to say, it wasn't easy.

Together with others who repeated the class, we were all subjected to ridicule. The greatest ridicule came from my Maths and Science teacher, whose subjects I failed and were the reason I had to repeat the class. At first it hurt to be reminded that we were "over age" for Matric at a Secondary School.

That year, the Department of Education had introduced what were called Finishing Schools. These were meant for students who were above the age of 18 and needed to rewrite Matric. In these schools, you only focused on the subjects you needed to repeat or upgrade to qualify for the course of your choice post High School.

I was turning 19 that year and was prepared to repeat the entire grade. I chose to ignore this teacher and made fun of my situation. I used to joke that I wanted a Master's Degree in Matric. At the end of that year, I was among those who passed. Though I did not obtain a 'master's degree', I did get better results than I did the first time. I passed both Maths and Science, obtained a distinction for Vernacular (Zulu) and a "B" for English which were important for my career choice, Public Relations.

REFLECTION

What stood out for me in this chapter

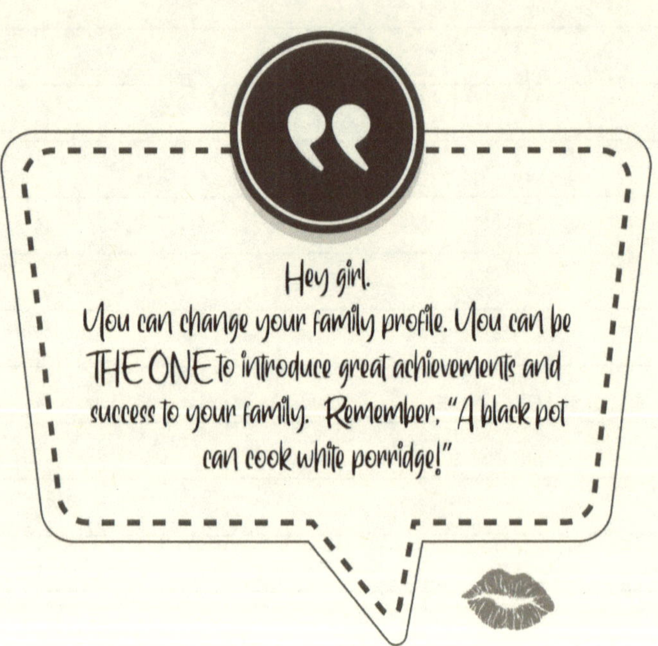
Hey girl.
You can change your family profile. You can be THE ONE to introduce great achievements and success to your family. Remember, "A black pot can cook white porridge!"

Chapter 2

WHO'S YOUR DADDY?

Father to the fatherless, defender of widows this is God, whose dwelling is holy

Psalm 68:5-6 New Living Translation (NLT)

January 2001 marked a new beginning in my life. I was done with 13 years of basic education and got introduced to a new world of higher education as a first year Public Relations student at the Technikon Witwatersrand (now University of Johannesburg).

All the friends I had in high school had gone to other institutions. I had no friends, struggled with transport money to commute between home and school. If I wasn't knocking on neighbours' doors to borrow R5 daily for a single train trip to school, I would stand at the train station hoping to meet someone I knew who could assist with money to buy a train ticket. Most of the time I would be able to raise R5. After school, I would wait until late so that the Ticket Officers would knock off. They used to knock off at 6pm. After 6pm, I could board the train for 'free'. The routine continued. Every morning, I knocked on neighbours' doors. When I failed, I would stand at the train station for someone to assist.

Transport money was not my only challenge. I needed textbooks and other items to support my new academic journey. Not having money for lunch did not bother me. I was used to starving. In fact my high school friends and I used to decide to fast when we didn't have food to eat. We used lunch breaks to pray for the school and ourselves. So being in Tertiary and attending lectures on an empty stomach was not a big deal. It was the other needs that pressed me so hard and made me need a father's help.

For the first time in my life, I decided to embark on a search for my father, a man I had never met. My mother's reluctance to answer any questions relating to him never motivated me to search for him or know more about him. However, in 2001, I convinced myself that I had to find him. The sudden motivation was not so much that I needed a father. After all, I had lived 20 years without knowing him. The cost of being a first-year student at a tertiary institution made me feel that it was about time I found him and somehow convince him to take financial responsibility of me. Unfortunately, my search was in vain. I never found him.

Yes, I was disappointed and anxious. It was never my dream to complete Matric and get employed immediately, I wanted more. With all the financial demands of tertiary education, it felt like I was chasing an impossible dream. In February 2001, I attended my church, Rhema Bible Church's Annual Conference. One of the guest speakers was an American Bishop who was speaking at our church for the first time. Before he started preaching, he asked everyone who was not raised by their fathers to stand up. I was among those who stood up. He said, "God is saying to you. "I did not trust your father enough to raise you, so I will raise you up Myself". That blew my mind and brought a certain calm. It shifted my focus from looking for my father to take care of me, to focusing on another Father who had assured me of His eternal presence, God. I figured, if my biological father really wanted to be a part of our lives, he would.

I thank God for a dear friend whom I met a few months into tertiary, Florence Khumalo. She literally took care of me. She bought me lunch at school, gave me transport money, allowed me to use her textbooks. She shared her clothes. She allowed me to squat in her room in the student residence during exams.

My tuition fee for the first year was partly covered by my church and the rest was from the Government's National Student Financial Aid Scheme (NSFAS). I decided that would be the only year where my studies would be financed through a loan. Though I had no clue where the finances for the rest of my course would come from, I had faith that God would make a way.

At the end of 2001, I reluctantly applied for a bursary advertised by the Gauteng Provincial Government.

According to my knowledge then, priority was given to students of Science and Accounting. I was in the Humanities stream. Being called for a shortlisting interview at the beginning of 2002 came as a surprise for me. January ended then February ended and March came to an end without feedback from the bursary interview. During this time, I continued attending lectures without an official registration. I convinced the lecturers that my name was not on the list of registered students because of an "Administration error". I could write tests and submit assignments for the entire term. Schools closed for Easter holidays. A few days before schools reopened, nerves started to kick in.

My story of the administration error was not going to hold water in the second term. I started imagining being denied access to school. I thought of how many people would laugh at me for being "ambitious". A part of me started questioning whether it was wise for me to not have applied for financial assistance through the NSFAS as I did in the first year.

April 2002, the holidays were over. I remember the day before schools re-opened, I went crying in prayer, feeling let down by God. The day schools re-opened, I decided to go to school and face being evicted. I attended the lectures for the "last time". When I returned home, I got the biggest and most pleasant surprise, a letter confirming the success of my bursary application. I was one of ten students who succeeded among thousands who applied for the bursary. Yes, my academic record was excellent. However, I believe there were some who got better results than I did. I just had the backing and favour from a Father who made a promise to me. From the second year of study until I graduated, my studies were financed by the Gauteng Provincial Government. Over 50% of the money I owed NSFAS was paid by an anonymous sponsor.

After all the hurdles and hard work, it was a proud moment for me to obtain my National Diploma in Public Relations, making me the first graduate in my family.

From that time, I have never been unemployed. By the time I graduated, I was employed full time in my field of study. The exposure to a life the word of God promised, became the hope that anchored my life.

I know that my story of an absent father is not unique. A lot of people do not know their fathers. I have seen how women especially young ones get into wrong relationships for provision. You may be one of them. I hope from my experience, you will discover that there is a God, who is THE FATHER. He can orchestrate help for you if you ask Him. You do not need a sugar daddy to make it in life. You do not need a "blesser" to advance. You don't need to drop your skirt to get employed.

REFLECTION

What stood out for me in this chapter

I've called your name.

You're mine. (Isaiah 43v 1)

Hey girl.
You may have not chosen where you were born.
Your parents may have abandoned or neglected you.
You can make a choice to not let it define you. Let your creator, God, define you. Yes, our families are a vehicle of entry to the world but ultimately, we belong to God.

Chapter 3

YOU ARE NOT YOUR PAIN

Forget about what's happened: don't keep going over old history. Be alert. Be present. I am about to do something brand new

Isaiah 43:18. (The Message Bible)

One of the most painful experiences I have ever had was being molested as a child. First, by a family friend and later, on numerous occasions, by a relative. This left me with deep scars especially as a young Christian girl who desired to remain a virgin until marriage. I lived with the confusion of whether God still viewed me as a virgin or not. Beyond that, I carried resentment against the adults who were supposed to protect me and didn't.

I was particularly angry at my mother whose absence, I believed, exposed me to hurt and abuse. There was a time in my life where her absence did not bother me. My mom had a habit of leaving for months without communicating her whereabouts. My grandmother, her mom, would worry sometimes not knowing if she would return as usual or if something had happened to her. Her friends would say she was staying somewhere in Alexandra.

One of my friends, Kgomotso Dladla, used to encourage me to find her. I suppose it did not make sense to her for a girl child to nonchalantly live her life without caring about her mother's whereabouts and presence. For a greater part of my childhood, my mom was an enemy in my heart. Whenever she was around, I treated her with great hostility and contempt.

My grandmother died in May 2001. After her burial, there was a bit of stability in my mother's presence, yet our relationship did not improve. I tolerated her.

The 1st of February 2004 is a day I will never forget. That's the day I had a showdown with her. It was a Sunday and I was home from church, and looking for the slip-on shoes I normally wore to rest my feet from high heels. I could not find them. I continued to search. On enquiry, I was told my mom was wearing them and she was sitting with her friend in one of the rooms outside the main house. I stormed into that room like something was chasing me. How dare she wore my shoes when she used to abandon us! Did she even know how much they cost? I embarrassed her in front of her friend. I rudely removed MY shoes from her feet. I screamed at her without caring about who was listening. For the first time, I expressed my disappointment and hurt about her absence and everything that surrounded it. For a moment, I forgot the 25 years age gap between us. I forgot about the honour I was supposed to bestow upon her. For me, everything that had to be said had to be said at that moment.

My mother was not quiet the entire time. She also gave me a piece of her mind. She told me how disappointed at the kind of Christian I was, how I respected everyone else but her despite having been the one who brought me to this world. She told me she did not have a problem disowning me since I seemed to have a lot of other "mothers". She told me she didn't want anything to do with me. I told her I didn't care since she was hardly ever there in the first place. I remember my younger brother walking in on that screaming match. I was hoping he would join me in telling our mother the 'truth', but he was not interested in joining in. All he wanted was for us to stop the screaming. I still don't know how my mother did not slap me that day. Though she did not beat me up, hearing her say she did not want anything to do with me hurt more than any slap would.

I could not sleep well that night. I asked myself if indeed I was a bad Christian. Was I really a bad daughter who deserved to be disowned? I knew my mom had the capacity to hold grudges. I saw how she dealt with her anger towards some of our relatives. Whenever they disagreed, she would bring up issues that were decades old, so I knew she meant what she said. I was okay being angry with her, but I could not handle her being angry with me.

Our exchange dominated my mind for most of that night. Morning came and it was awkward in the house. I didn't know whether to greet her or not. I didn't know if we would have another showdown. I was feeling embarrassed especially as I realised that the issue was not even the shoes. Those shoes cost me less than R200 and I was employed at that time.

The shoes became a convenient opportunity let out what I had been harbouring inside. I could not continue like nothing happened. I decided not to go to work. I could not immediately apologise to my mother but could not ignore the conviction in my heart. I greeted her and she ignored me. I told her the reason I didn't go to work was because I had planned an outing for us. That was not true, but she warmed up to that and agreed to go with me to eat at a restaurant. I apologised to her. She accepted my apology and told me that we should strive not to make our "enemies" happy.

I thank God for the conviction and the healing and freedom that came from eventually forgiving and mending things with her. We forgave each other but we didn't become best of friends. That was the only outing we had. She was still my mother and I was still her daughter. Now that I am older, I have more empathy for her journey and experiences. I look back and I can conclude that my mother had her own brokenness. Five children from four different men. Never married. No decent education. Mainly domestic work. I used to judge her but now I have some compassion for her. Alcohol abuse and her lifestyle were probably a way of medicating herself. We never had a conversation about it. I am just glad that by the time she passed away in 2009, she was a born again Christian and I know I will meet her in heaven someday.

My experience may be light in comparison with what you may have experienced in your life's journey. You may have been betrayed and rejected. You may have poured yourself in a relationship that left you wounded. Whatever the case is, the reality is that you cannot always control how other people treat you. People will hurt you knowingly and unknowingly. Your part is choosing how you react and deal with the hurt.

"See to it that no one falls short of God's grace; that no root of resentment springs up and causes trouble, and by it many be defiled" Hebrews 12:15 (AMP)

Bitterness is birthed through prolonged, unresolved offence. Focusing on my mom and my disappointment with her blinded me from seeing that my heart had become so ugly. I put the spotlight on her and ignored my own bitterness. Maybe yours is not an emotional pain. It could perhaps be a long-standing physical pain or condition that has left you with limited functionality. It could be a condition that has attracted a label that you don't like.

Sometimes the pain is not in its intensity but in how long it persists. Luke 12 makes mention of a woman who suffered an issue of blood for 12 years.

According to scripture, she had spent all her money trying to get medical help to no avail.

Every woman goes through an "issue of blood" regularly and in most cases there's no cause for concern. But 12 years? I don't know the conversations she had with herself throughout the time. I don't know the whispers that went on around her about her condition. Is it not amazing how people have 'insight' about why others are experiencing what they are experiencing? Is it not amazing how easy it is for people to point at you and suggest that you invited the pain one way or the other without checking the facts? I don't know the circumstances that surrounded this woman. All I know is when her faith connected with the power and the compassion of Jesus, there was an immediate change in her situation. I have interacted with enough people to know that everyone has an issue. It may not be an issue of blood but there is an issue everyone has that needs the attention and the power of God. There is no doubt that God can deal with any kind of challenge. The question is, have you allowed the persistence of your difficulty to convince you that there is no hope? Have you convinced yourself that the limitation of human help means there is no help for you?

I wonder what went on this woman's mind moments before she touched the helm of Jesus' garment. My imagination tells me that there was a moment when she had a flashback of her visits to the best physicians only to get disappointed. I am happy that if she indeed had those flashbacks, her hunger and desperation for change propelled her to push through the crowd and meet with her help.

This reminds me of another passage in the Bible. The story of a blind man called Bartimeus. A man who was known to stand at the corner of the street, begging. On one day, blind Bartimeus heard that Jesus was in town and started shouting for His help. What caught my attention in the story of Bartimeus is Jesus' response to his crying. Jesus asked

Bartimeus, "What do you want me to do for you?" The same Jesus who could read the minds of Pharisees asked the obviously blind man, "What do you want me to do for you?"

Was it not obvious what he needed?

I don't believe Jesus asked the question because He didn't know Bartimeus' need. I believe the real question was, "Bartimeus, do you believe I can help you and do you give me permission to do something about your status?"

The question is still valid today. I've been in church services where the Pastor would say, "God is here, ask Him anything you want Him to do for you". I must admit, there have been instances where I froze at that command. It wasn't because I didn't have needs and it certainly wasn't because I don't believe God is able. The issue has been not being able to articulate my expectation. You can know your need and God can see your need, yet nothing will happen without a clearly articulated expectation.

"Expectation is the mother of manifestation"! God, even in His infinite power, works within the parameters of our expectation. That same question is still relevant today: "What do you want Me to do for you?"

Broken woman, what do you want Me to do for you? Insecure woman, what do you want Me to do for you?"

What do you want Him to do for you?

Get rid of all bitterness, rage, anger, harsh words, and slander, as well as all types of evil behaviour. Instead, be kind to each other, tender-hearted, forgiving one another, just as God through Christ has forgiven you.

Ephesians 4:31-32 (NLT)

REFLECTION

What stood out for me in this chapter

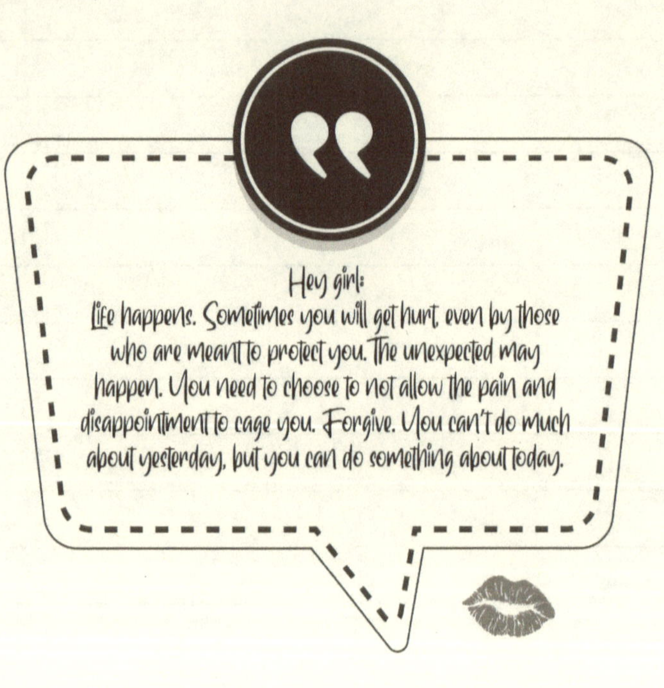
Hey girl:
Life happens. Sometimes you will get hurt, even by those who are meant to protect you. The unexpected may happen. You need to choose to not allow the pain and disappointment to cage you. Forgive. You can't do much about yesterday, but you can do something about today.

Chapter 4

ONE OF A KIND

Oh yes! You shaped me first inside then out: you formed me in my mother's womb... You know me inside and out: you know every bone in my body. You know exactly how I was made, bit by bit, how I was sculpted from nothing into something. Like an open book, you watched me grow from conception to birth: all the stages of my life were spread out before you, the days of my life all prepared before I'd even lived one day

Psalms 139v13-16: The Message Bible

I am generally not a shy person. I don't remember having been. Yes, I exercise restraint when necessary, but I am not shy. Throughout my life, if I was not in the choir, I was debating. If not, I was participating in a play, performing a poem or being a speaker, motivating or directing a programme.

As early as primary school days, in one way or the other, leadership responsibilities followed me whether as a class representative, a member of the Student Representative Council Executive, leading our church's home fellowship group, the youth, the choir and many more.

Externally, I have always been bold yet, for a while, I was insecure about my body. In my eyes I was not attractive. Gifted, yes! But not attractive. One of my body features that used to receive negative comments was my 'abundant' behind. Even when I was thin, that part of my body always stood out.

Some of my peers used to call me "gogo" (granny). I think this was also because of the kind of clothes I used to wear. Most of them were donated by neighbours, church and my teachers. In my teenage years, I gained a lot of weight so some of the adult clothes could fit me. This probably justified me being called gogo. However, it added to my feelings of unattractiveness. My gifts and academic prowess became my strength. Except for sport, I have always been in the front. I have always been among those chosen to lead, represent, and be part of something significant, including the Children's Parliament hosted by the Gauteng Provincial Legislature.

I remember how I used to divert any compliment that related to my physique because I did not believe it. One of my friends, Mathapelo Nhlapo, used to compliment my smile and for a long time, I thought she was just being kind because she was my friend. She would always find something to compliment about my body. With her compliments and regular teachings from my church's young women's fellowships, I began to believe that indeed I AM BEAUTIFUL. I learnt to accept my body as it is. I learnt to accept that I am one of a kind, that there is no one like me in the entire world. That is one of the wonders about how God created human beings. You are nobody's copy. I look at my children. Both come from my womb, have the same father yet they are so different. Each has their own personality and carries a specific assignment. Your power lies in the fact that you have something nobody else has. You are uniquely created regardless of the package you come in.

Don't allow other people's views of you determine how you feel about yourself. Don't allow anyone or anything to make you believe you have nothing to offer this world. The truth is, God has loaded you with enough ability for you to be you. You and I are created in the image of God. God put His best in us! Celebrate yourself and every ability God has loaded you with.

You do not have to compete with anyone. We are built differently. Our gifts, callings and skills are different in function not in significance. That someone else looks different and can do what you cannot do does not mean they carry more value than you. Someone may match your name, weight, age, but you still have a unique set of fingerprints that distinguish you from every other person including your twin if you have one. Appreciate yourself. I have made peace with the fact that I am one of a kind, that there's no spare me somewhere, that there's a role ONLY I can play on this earth. My looks and people's opinions don't define me. I am determined to make a mark.

One of the areas I am committed to making a mark, is in my role as a parent. I am committed to affirm my children, especially my daughter; with regards to her body and her looks in general. Being dark in completion among school friends who are lighter and thinner than her, she informed me about how others at school tease her. My response has always been, "They are blind, they can't see how beautiful you are". I never miss an opportunity to tell her about her beauty and her kind heart. I can't control what others do or say to her. All I can do is to be a positive influence on how she sees herself.

For we are God's masterpiece. He has created us anew in Christ Jesus, so we can do the good things he planned for us long ago.

Ephesians 2:10 (NLT)

REFLECTION

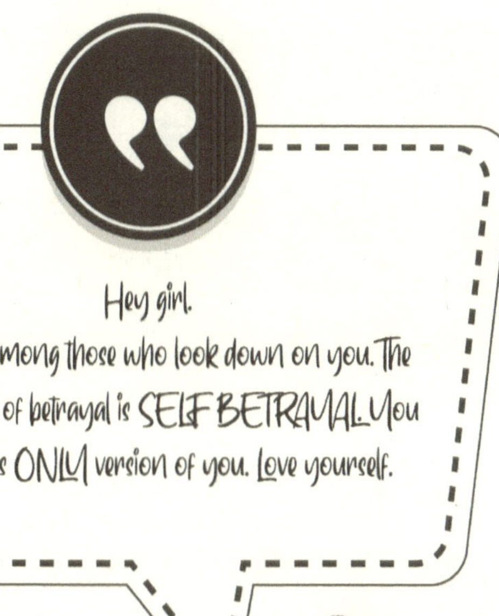
Hey girl.
Don't be among those who look down on you. The worst form of betrayal is SELF BETRAYAL. You are God's ONLY version of you. Love yourself.

Chapter 5

NO MORE SHAME

Fear not; you will no longer live in shame. Don't be afraid; there is no more disgrace for you. You will no longer remember the shame of your youth and the sorrows of widowhood

Isaiah 54:4 (New Living Translation)

Have you ever been in a situation where you felt like the earth should just open and swallow you? Where you thought you can't face another day or people because of the strong feeling of shame? October 2009 stands out for me as the day those feelings were the most intense. I had to make a phone call to announce to my Pastor that I was pregnant. This was a big deal as I was unmarried at the time and I was leader at church. I was not proud of myself, especially having preached no sex before marriage. I was a, "No ringy, no dingy" advocate.

All sorts of thoughts went through my head. What will everyone say? What will my family say? Fortunately for me, I did not get the tongue lashing and the condemnation I thought I would get; yet that didn't immediately remove the guilt and the consciousness of having deviated from God's principles. That's what shame does. Instead of feeling bad about our actions, shame makes you feel bad about who you are. Shame is defined as a "painful feeling of humiliation or distress caused by the consciousness of wrong or foolish behaviour".

The love I received from both my family and church blew my mind. Even when I felt unworthy, I was lavished with love. I could continue participating in church as a leader. It also helped that my boyfriend, who is now my husband, did not run away from his responsibility. While I was panicking, he was ecstatic. To him, the pregnancy was a gift from God, and he embraced it unreservedly. This gesture helped me to get back on my feet. I was able to embrace my new journey as a mother.

Sadly, not everyone experiences the same embrace when they do wrong. We live in a judgemental society. I have seen how relationships changed because of "falling from grace". I have seen how some who come to church with a pregnancy without a husband receive "looks" from those who are not in the same situation.

The judgemental attitude is nothing new. Who can forget the story of the woman who was caught in an act of adultery in the Bible and was brought before Jesus?

"Jesus returned to the Mount of Olives, but early the next morning he was back again at the Temple. A crowd soon gathered, and he sat down and taught them. As he was speaking, the teachers of religious law and the Pharisees brought a woman who had been caught in the act of adultery. They put her in front of the crowd. Teacher," they said to Jesus, "this woman was caught in the act of adultery. The law of Moses says to stone her. What do you say?" They

were trying to trap him into saying something they could use against him, but Jesus stooped down and wrote in the dust with his finger. They kept demanding an answer, so he stood up again and said, "All right, but let the one who has never sinned throw the first stone!" Then he stooped down again and wrote in the dust. When the accusers heard this, they slipped away one by one, beginning with the oldest, until only Jesus was left in the middle of the crowd with the woman. Then Jesus stood up again and said to the woman, "Where are your accusers? Didn't even one of them condemn you?" "No, Lord," she said. And Jesus said, "Neither do I. Go and sin no more." John 8:1-11 New Living Translation (NLT)

She was dragged to Jesus whom they expected to further humiliate her. Instead, His compassion reached out to her. "Neither do I (condemn you)". Essentially, He was saying, "You did something wrong, but I still love you. Don't do it again. Learn from this mistake".

You are forgiven. Even when we know this, we sometimes let the memory of our wrongdoing disable us. Psychologists have noted a close relationship between shame and suicide.

That's the extent of shame's toxicity.

Failing can also be a source of shame. Though we don't plan to fail, failure happens to most us at one moment or the other. Failure in business, school, relationships and so on. Sometimes failure comes as a spiritual attack. Other times, it comes as a result of our carelessness or lack of wisdom in some areas.

The worst part about failure is having a constant reminder of where you've failed. You may be familiar with labels like, "divorcee", "ex-drug addict", "ex-convict" and so on. Sometimes we put those labels on ourselves because of how much we feel we have let ourselves down. Important as it is to ignore negative words from others, what you say to yourself is extremely important. Sometimes you need to bang the door against the memory of failure. Bang the door against the memory of disappointment and press forward. In his book, "Failing Forward", (Thomas Nelson Publishers, 2007), John C Maxwell makes the following statement about failure: "The more you do, the more you fail. The more you fail, the more you learn. The more you learn, the better you get". Don't focus on the failure, focus on the lesson.

Encourage yourself! Speak words that inspire life. The truth is, EVERYONE has issues to deal with. FIGHT and WIN! I like what Apostle Paul says,

"I am not saying that I have this all together, that I have made it. But I am well on my way, reaching out for Christ, who has so wondrously reached out for me. Friends, don't get me wrong: By no means do I count myself an expert in all of this, but I've got my eye on the goal, where God is beckoning us onward—to Jesus. I'm off and running, and I'm not turning back." Philippians 3:12-14 (The Message Bible)

REFLECTION

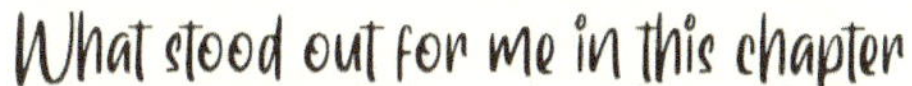

If we claim we have no sin, we are only fooling ourselves and not living in the truth. But if we confess our sins to him, he is faithful and just to forgive us our sins and to cleanse us from all wickedness.

1 John 1:8-9 (NLT)

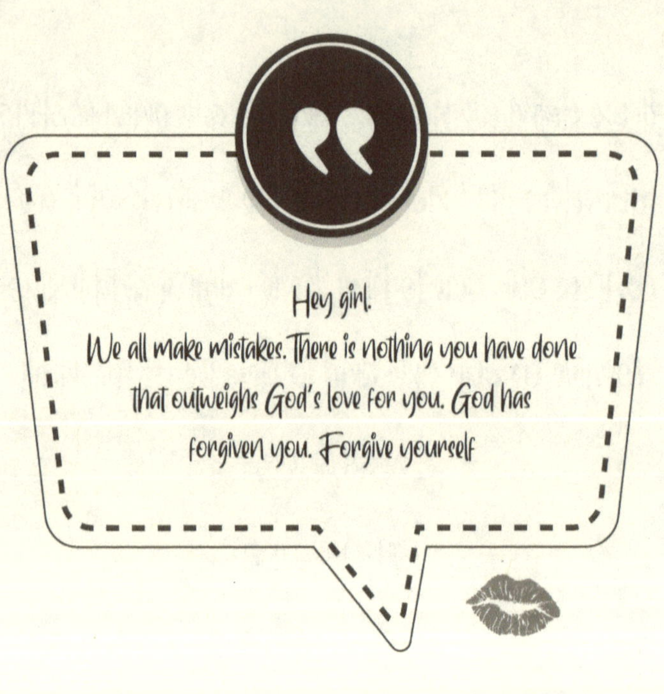
Hey girl.
We all make mistakes. There is nothing you have done
that outweighs God's love for you. God has
forgiven you. Forgive yourself

Chapter 6

INTO ME SEE

Now that we know what we have Jesus, this great High Priest with ready access to God let's not let it slip through our fingers. We don't have a priest who is out of touch with our reality. He's been through weakness and testing, experienced it all but the sin. So, let's walk right up to him and get what He is so ready to give.

Take the mercy, accept the help

Hebrews 4: 16 The Message Bible

There are some struggles and issues so deep and private that make you wonder, "Can I say this to a Holy God? Can I open my mouth about my addictions, about my unholy habits to a God who is Holy?

As a young Christian, I was used to having regular conversations with God through prayer. This relationship carried on through to my teenage years and beyond. I prayed about anything and everything except for this one thing - my battle with masturbation.

I believe my molestation by a relative opened the door to this habit. Unlike the first incident with a family friend when I was much younger that happened once, this one happened in my early teens on repeated occasions. I remember how this relative would wait until everyone was asleep, roll himself close to me (we used to sleep on lounge floor in my mother's aunt's lounge because the house was too small). He would pull my hand to touch him and did the same to me. I reported this repeatedly and it took a while for his father to address him. I never received an apology. I decided to release both the family friend and my relative from my heart. I decided not to hold their deeds against them.

Though the abuse stopped, my body was used to "stimulation". I resorted to masturbating. I know there are a lot of beliefs and medical justification for this habit. For me, this is totally against my convictions and it made me feel terrible. I would repent but still go back. Every time I went back, I was uncomfortable to pray because I felt like a spotlight of judgement was on me. Though I still went to church, I battled to connect with God during the services. My conversations with God were dominated by continuous apologies.

Sometime in the 90s, Hillsong and Alvin Slaughter released a song, "I will run to you". The chorus says,

"I will run to you. To your words of truth.

Not by might. Not by power. But by the spirit of God.

I will run the race, 'till I see your face. Let me live in the glory of your grace".

This became my anthem. My refuge song. A song that invited an imperfect me to the presence of a Holy God. I stopped running from Him and ran to Him. I did not stop this habit immediately. In fact, it took a long while. When I stopped hiding, I was able to pray about it with a lesser feeling of judgement. I would go back to it but continued to pray until I was able to overcome the urge.

Sin and brokenness can make you hide. I have seen how a lot of people turned their backs against God because they could not face Him. You do not have to. Jesus empathises with our weaknesses. The whole mandate Jesus came to fulfil was reaching out to the broken, imperfect people like you and me.

"The Spirit of the Lord is upon Me, Because He has anointed Me To preach the gospel to the poor; He has sent Me to heal the broken-hearted, To proclaim liberty to the captives And recovery of sight to the blind, To set at liberty those who are oppressed; To proclaim the acceptable year of the Lord." (Luke 4v18-19, NKJV).

A line from one of Bette Middler's songs says, "God is watching us from a distance". I'm not sure what she meant. All I know is that God has never intended to be a distant God. He always wanted fellowship with man. Central to my healing and confidence is the intimate relationship I've had with God.

Bishop TD Jakes defines intimacy as **"INTO-ME-SEE"**. Where you can present yourself, "warts and all" It is the type of closeness that even silent communication can be interpreted by the other party.

The dilemma for most people is: "how do I relate to a God I have never seen, a God I cannot touch?" Intimacy does not happen overnight. God reveals Himself to us primarily through His word. We relate to God through what scripture tells us about Him. As you start believing His word, applying His word, speaking to Him through prayer and spending time in His presence, trust develops. It is difficult to be intimate with someone you do not trust. The same applies in our relationship with God. Intimacy develops as you begin to trust God and believe that He will never reject you and that His heart desires closeness to His children. Intimacy breeds confidence.

One of God's amazing attributes is His accessibility. A God who is majestic and holy came to the level of mankind not to judge but to draw man to Himself.

Accept the invitation of intimacy with a loving God.

"Look at me. I stand at the door. I knock. If you hear me call and open the door, I'll come right in and sit down to supper with you". (Revelations 3:20 - The Message Bible)

REFLECTION

What stood out for me in this chapter

Hey girl.
Don't allow anything to push you away from the
presence of God. He knows everything about you.
You don't have to hide from Him.

Chapter 7

MAY THE REAL YOU, PLEASE STAND UP!

So, here's what I want you to do, God helping you: Take your everyday, ordinary life your sleeping, eating, going-to-work, and walking-around life and place it before God as an offering. Embracing what God does for you is the best thing you can do for him. Don't become so well-adjusted to your culture that you fit into it without even thinking. Instead, fix your attention on God. You'll be changed from the inside out. Readily recognize what He wants from you, and quickly respond to it. Unlike the culture around you, always dragging you down to its level of immaturity, God brings the best out of you, develops well-formed maturity in you

(Romans 12:1-2 The Message Bible)

After my Matric Dance, the next time I wore make up was in 2004. A colleague of mine was selling make up products and offered to do my face. I agreed. It was during the week, just after we knocked off. When I got home, one of my brothers asked me why I was disguising. His message was loud and clear. What was meant to enhance looked like a disguise.

For a long time, humour was my disguise. I would find a way to escape seriousness in relation to my emotions, especially when it is negative emotions. There was a time when I would never cry in front of people because to me that exposed my weakness. I was first to comfort others. I was the superhero, yet I found heart-to-heart conversations very intimidating.

One of the people God used to remove my mask was my friend Florence. She is the master of heart to heart. I remember how she would stare at me during conversations like she was reading my soul. She encouraged me to cry when I needed to. She would ask the most awkward questions to get to the core of whatever I was avoiding discussing. At first it was very uncomfortable. I felt that she was too much. I was okay discussing any general issue but not the issues of my heart. As our relationship grew, I got to trust her and opened up more.

One of the things I treasure about my relationship with Florence is understanding that I am not perfect, that expressing pain is not a sign of weakness but an attribute of being human. Now, I laugh, I cry, I get angry, I still joke with freedom. I am not concerned about who is watching. I don't have to fake strength when I feel weak. I don't have to go out of my way to crack a joke do divert my pain.

What is your disguise?

It is so easy to fake it in the environment we are living in, where our minds are fed with images, information, trends and values on a 24-hour basis through a variety of media. Those of us who are on social media can attest to how 'perfect' people's lives are portrayed on these platforms. In general, we only post about the positives in our lives: the lovely car, the beautiful house, the loving partner, the perfectly cooked food, the flawless faces and hair.

We find ourselves spending time staring at other people's lives, achievements, and possessions not for inspiration but to compare ourselves with them and imitate them in some instances. Staring at people's "perfect" lives can make you believe that something is wrong with yours. Women have bleached their skin, undergone painful cosmetic surgery to alter their bodies to look like other people. It is rare that we post our real issues and struggles.

I do not support and encourage those who use social media to vent or air their dirty laundry. However, you don't have to portray a false life. The reality is a lot of people exaggerate or lie on social media. Fake it 'till you make it, has become the accepted trend.

Why? Why should you go out of your way to be who you are not? What is wrong with not owning a Louis Vuitton bag, a Gucci item? Why do we go out of our way to buy fake items? What is wrong with accepting the level that you are on? I am a believer in aspiring for the best and working for the best. However, when you are on your way there, make sure you don't leave the REAL YOU behind.

REFLECTION

What stood out for me in this chapter

"Authenticity; the courage to be yourself"-
Anonymous

God has given each of you a gift from his great variety of spiritual gifts. Use them well to serve one another.

1 Peter 4:10 New Living Translation (NLT

Hey girl.
It is okay to have role models. Learn from others but remain an original. Don't be swallowed by the need to be 'liked', especially on social media. Always do YOU!

Chapter 8

JUST DO IT

Dear friends, do you think you'll get anywhere in this if you learn all the right words but never do anything? Does merely talking about faith indicate that a person really has it?

James 2v14 (The Message)

I have a concern about absent fathers. It bothers me when men impregnate women and walk away, when women use their bitterness to prevent men to father their children. I am aware of the different dynamics around the issue of absent fathers however it still bothers me. This is primarily because of my first-hand experience of not having a father. The concern I have led me to initiate an event called, *"Dance with my father"*.

The event is aimed at encouraging active fatherhood and to fostering closeness between fathers and their daughters. It is also to communicate that not every father is a runaway dad. Not every father is an abuser. I have watched the relationship my husband has with our daughter, the love, attention, affection and how he makes sure he provides for her. That's my desire for every girl: A stable, secure relationship with their fathers.

I have received feedback on how the Dance with my father event is a highlight for some families, how girls look forward to a day when they would have uninterrupted time spent with the fathers. I have been told how this event has enhanced closeness between fathers and their girls.

I had obstacles along the way, mainly in the area of funding. I have been discouraged and contemplated quitting. I am glad I did not. Since 2016, we have not skipped a year without hosting the event.

This is my vision. My dream. What is yours? What are you doing with the dreams and desires that are burning in your heart? Think about those dreams that you've carried in your heart as a child. What happened to them? Why have you not pursued them?

One of my childhood dreams was to write a book. In fact, when I was in High school, I wrote 'biographies' for two of my friends, Mathapelo Nhlapo and Tumelo Nkosi. Yes, they were handwritten and not up to scratch but even then,

I knew one of the things I must accomplish before the end of my life is writing books.

I must however confess that even with my passion and skill for writing, as I put this book together, I went through insecurity. I compared myself with "accomplished writers" and I immediately felt intimidated. But you see, if I had given in to that fear, I would not have continued. I would have suppressed my passion because of feeling like I can't match others' standard. I am certain that you have also felt the same way or are still feeling the same way, fearful and intimidated. But you know what? Just do it. Throw yourself to it.

No matter the size of your dream, if YOU don't make up your mind to put it into action, nothing will happen. "Faith without action is dead"!

Fear can paralyse you. If you don't master fear, it will master you. God has availed Himself to be our help. It is recorded that the words, "Fear not" are written 365 times in the Bible. How amazing is that. That means you and I have heaven's backing every day of our lives. This is enough motivation to pursue all those dreams you have buried in your heart.

There is a term I recently heard; God-fidence. It is defined as *"an assurance of mind and a firm belief in the reality of God, and possessing the courage to completely become who God has called you to be, and do what He has called you to do"*.

Don't panic. I'm with you.

There's no need to fear for I'm your God.

I'll give you strength. I'll help you.

Isaiah 41:10 (The Message Bible)

REFLECTION

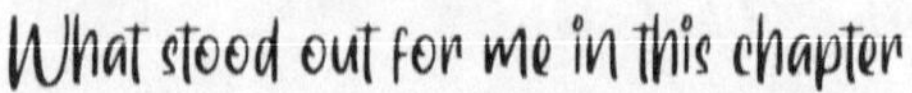

Hey girl.

You need to learn to doubt your doubts. Don't listen to the voice of fear. Go for that thing you have always wanted to do. Once you are at it, you will realise there was really nothing to fear

Chapter 9

HOW FAR CAN YOU SEE?

After Lot separated from him, God said to Abram, Open your eyes, look around. Look north, south, east, and west. Everything you see, the whole land spread out before you, I will give to you and your children forever.

Genesis 13v14-15 (The Message Bible)

THE POWER OF VISION

The Bible says, *"Without a vision, people perish".*

A life lived without a vision is a killer of potential. It does not matter how much ability you have, if you do not do anything about it, it will not benefit you or anyone else for that matter.

I like the definition that says, "vision is the ability to think about or plan the future with imagination or wisdom".

One of the things that can happen to you when you are from a disadvantaged background is to believe that you don't qualify for the best, that only a certain class of people can attain greatness. I grew up hearing (and still do) the statement, "izinto zabelungu" directly translated as "white people's things". This statement is usually made to refer to anything of excellent quality. It could be a house, a car, cell phone, food. It implies that if you are not white, you can't be associated with a certain level of quality and excellence. This is unfortunately a mindset that has kept a lot of people in mediocrity. The Bible says, as a man thinks, so is he. Your life moves towards the direction of your thoughts. "Both the one who thinks they can and the one who thinks they can't, are right".

My friend Tumelo and I came from similar backgrounds of lack. As young girls, all we had was the word of God, imagination and faith. We used to sit and talk about the future we wanted. We made plans even knowing that we did not have financial backing.

We imagined ourselves with tertiary qualifications without financial backing from our families. We imagined hosting a HUGE graduation party to celebrate our achievement while sitting without lunch during school breaks. Fast forward, we both attained our qualifications. We hosted the graduation party we dreamt about. We both are in our careers of choice. I have concluded that faith and vision level the playing field. These two are not determined by your status. Both the poor and the rich can have faith and vision. With these two, you can break barriers.

As the years go by, I am learning that vision keeps your spirit alive. It energises you and gives you a reason to hope and to carry on.

Vision simplifies your life and limits your choices.

Somethings are not inherently bad but may not be good for you because they conflict with your vision. *"Everything is permissible but not everything is beneficial!"*

There are people I have cut off from my life not because they are evil but because they are not relevant to where I'm going. I had to limit my interaction with them until we grew apart.

If you don't have a vision, you'll be controlled by people's opinions and suggestions. You will be controlled by trends. As the saying goes *"If you don't know where you are going, any road will lead you there"*

Ladies in general, love to be in relationships. We like to connect with others. Have you asked yourself why you are friends with those you are friends with? What do you and your friends have in common? What value are your relationships adding to your life and vision? Are you adding any value to the people in your life?

"The Godly give good advice to their friends; the wicked lead them astray" Proverbs 12:26 (NLT)

"Become wise by walking with the wise; hang out with fools and watch your life fall to pieces". Proverbs 13:20 The Message Bible

One of my favourite speakers and author, Tim Storey defines a fool as, *"someone who lacks understanding on purpose".*

Meaning a fool is someone who chooses to ignore instruction or wisdom. **Be careful of such people in your life.**

REFLECTION

What stood out for me in this chapter

Hey girl.

Have you thought about where your life is going? It's important to think about it. That will help you in your choices. If you know where you are going, you can't make choices that are taking you the opposite direction from where you want to go.

Chapter 10

PRISON DOORS ARE OPEN

The Spirit of the Sovereign Lord is upon me, for the Lord has anointed me to bring good news to the poor.

He has sent me to comfort the broken hearted and to proclaim that captives will be released and prisoners will be freed.

Isaiah 61 New Living Translation (NLT)

There's a prison called, "This is how I am". It's a prison where bad attitudes, pessimism, cynicism and meanness live. Here, many close out the beauty of healthy relationships with others. Many shut the door against growth, against miracles, against love. It's not where you want to be found. I believe God has given us women an inborn tenderness. Sometimes too much exposure to pain and unkindness can erode that softness, making us to stop caring about others and their feelings. If you find yourself in that state, return to your Maker. Pray that He restores you. I remember a time when I was aggressive and somewhat a bully. I expected to have the last word. I believed my views were superior to others. I had an appetite for arguing and debating because I didn't like to be wrong. I saw this as strength and great leadership. Now I know that strength is not rude. You can be both polite and assertive.

I will not forget a moment as a leader of the youth in my church. We had a banquet and agreed on arrival time. One of the leaders arrived later than the agreed time. The way I screamed at him. I didn't care that he came with a guest. I did not even give him a chance to explain himself. He later told me how I made him feel and honestly, I was not bothered because in my eyes, he was wrong and had to be told BY ME. This incident led him to give me the nickname, "Margaret Thatcher". He had the courage to confront me.

Looking back, I have realised that my need to be right all the time was deeply rooted in my impaired self-esteem.

God has helped me through the years. I am amazed that one of the words people use to describe me now is, "calm." I have learned to be considerate of the feelings of others. I have learned to think about how to say what I need to say.

"And I will give you a new heart, and I will put a new spirit in you. I will take out your stony, stubborn heart and give you a tender, responsive heart". Ezekiel 36v:26 New Living Translation (NLT)

"Do nothing from selfishness or empty conceit [through factional motives, or strife], but with [an attitude of] humility [being neither arrogant nor self-righteous], regard others as more important than yourselves". Philippians 2:3 (AMP)

REFLECTION

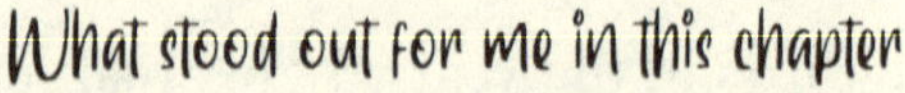

What stood out for me in this chapter

Therefore, as God's chosen people, holy and dearly loved, clothe yourselves with compassion, kindness, humility, gentleness and patience.

Colossians 3:12 (NIV)

Hey girl.

You don't have to arrest yourself. The real you is kind, tender-hearted and caring. Don't let a bad attitude lock you up. You don't have to be mean to "protect your heart". You are better than that.

Chapter 11

YOU ARE ENOUGH- EVEN WITHOUT THE RING

So, you also are complete through your union with Christ, who is the head over every ruler and authority

Colossians 2:10 (NLT

A lot of women dream about get married. I also dreamt about getting married. Even when I had not started dating, I daydreamed about possible surnames I could be married into. I went to an extent of practising my 'new signature' with my 'husband's' surname. In my mid-twenties, I started drafting a template of my dream wedding. I knew who the bridesmaids would be, Matron of Honour, the dress, the works. At the age of 29, I got married.

You may still be waiting, with or without a template. Sometimes being unmarried can bring unnecessary pressure. There are women who believe they are incomplete without the title, "Mrs" and that ring on their finger. But marriage does not define you neither does it increase your worth. According to the late Dr Myles Munroe, "Marriage is when two separate, unique and WHOLE people (one male, one female) make a covenant to exchange vows, committing their lives to remain together until death".

Desiring marriage to feel complete or to improve your self-esteem can leave you with untold loneliness and great disappointment. Bishop TD Jakes says, "To be married is to have a partner, someone who is not always there or always on target or always anything. If you are looking for someone to be your everything, don't look around, look up.

God is the only One who can be your EVERYTHING".

But Jesus said, "Not everyone is mature enough to live a married life. It requires a certain aptitude and grace. Marriage isn't for everyone. Some, from birth seemingly, never give marriage a thought. Others never get asked—or accepted. And some decide not to get married for kingdom reasons. But if you're capable of growing into the largeness of marriage, do it."

Matthew 19:11-12 The Message (MSG)

REFLECTION

What stood out for me in this chapter

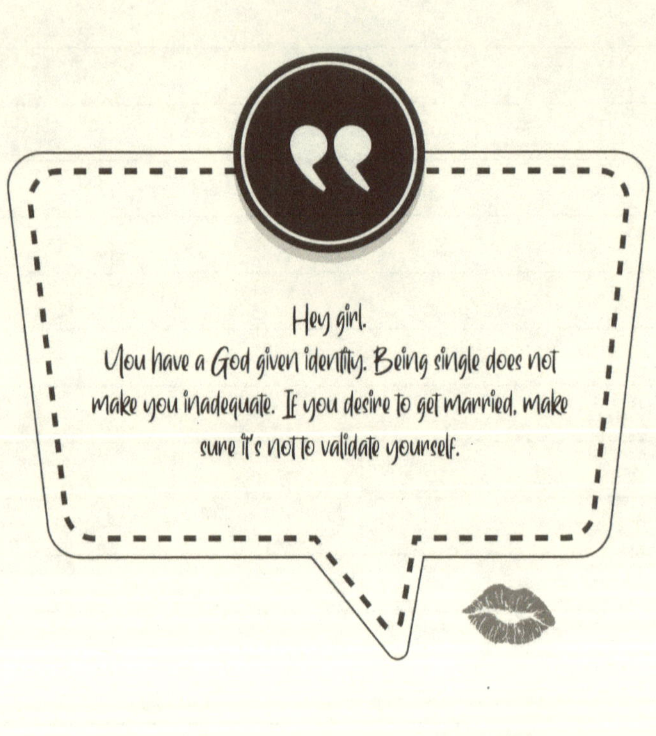
Hey girl.
You have a God given identity. Being single does not make you inadequate. If you desire to get married, make sure it's not to validate yourself.

CONCLUSION

Life demands a great deal of courage. Not just courage to face your fears but to live at peace with yourself even with exposed weaknesses, especially in a world of fake perfection. It takes courage to forgive yourself for living below your set standards, courage to be able to separate yourself from your mistakes.

It takes courage to lean towards kindness when you feel justified to be vindictive.

It takes courage to crawl towards your dreams amidst opposition, to be convinced of your worth in scarcity, to smile and dance in the storm.

It takes courage to look at each day with expectation that it could be THAT DAY you've prayed for.

My dear sisters, let us celebrate our strength and relevance in the plan of God for humanity. May God impress in our hearts our worth as His daughters in a world that is so hostile to women.

May the power of God erase every painful memory that has built walls around our hearts, disabling us from expressing our inborn tenderness.

May God erase every memory of failure that has kept us bound in fear to pursue the dreams that God has engraved in our hearts.

May we be filled with compassion for ourselves for times when we are not able to be the best mothers, the best wives, daughters, sisters, friends that we would love to be.

May we accept that even with our flaws, we are still adequate. Even with our issues, we are still God's beloved.

Even with our regrets, we are still forgiven. Overall, we are all that!

www.ingramcontent.com/pod-product-compliance
Lightning Source LLC
LaVergne TN
LVHW051005080826
845145LV00009B/2458

* 9 7 8 0 6 2 0 8 5 8 2 9 8 *